GROUNDBREAKING INTERVENTIONS:
Working with Traumatized Children, Teens and Families in Foster Care and Adoption

18 Interventions for Social Workers and Parents to heal Anxiety, Fear, Worry, Stress, Anger, Aggressivity, Frustration, Poor Impulse Control, Grief, Loss, and Depression. In order to build Self-esteem, Identity Formation, Family, Trust, Safety, Security, and Bonding with Attachment Challenged Children.

JEANETTE YOFFE, M.F.T.
www.CeliaCenter.org

ISBN: 978-1-300-78324-4 (sc)
ISBN: 978-1-4834-0959-7 (e)

Because of the dynamic nature of the Internet, any web addresses or links contained in
this book may have changed since publication and may no longer be valid. The views
expressed in this work are solely those of the author and do not necessarily reflect the
views of the publisher, and the publisher hereby disclaims any responsibility for them.

Any people depicted in stock imagery provided by Thinkstock are models,
and such images are being used for illustrative purposes only.
Certain stock imagery © Thinkstock.

Lulu Publishing Services rev. date: 08/07/2014

"Jeanette offers dozens of targeted tips that engage children through sensory experiences, play and creativity. The interventions require very little planning and are straightforward yet profound. They offer children the opportunity to directly and indirectly express to adults and to themselves their most coveted thoughts and feelings. Jeanette's empathy, experience and imagination are evident as she clearly explains each exercise. A must read/watch for anyone working with or raising children in foster care or adoption."

-**SHEILA KAMEN**, Ph.D. Psychologist and Foster-Adoptive Parent

"Hands on fantastic. Fabulous!"
"This is awesome. It really gave us practical, creative ways to help kids."
"Effective and efficient. Well developed and easy to use."

-**CLINICAL STAFF**, Jewish Family Services

"Jeanette's techniques have had such positive outcomes with the children and families she has worked with throughout the years. Her empathic and caring nature motivates the children to use the exercises, which help them to express what is going on for them. I highly recommend this book for anyone parenting or working with children in foster care or who have been adopted."

-**ROBYN HARROD**, L.C.S.W., Adoption Program Director

"Jeanette is the consummate professional. She possesses that rare combination of; an amazing sensitivity to her clients, experience, passion and skill. She is my number 1 recommendation for a psychotherapist specializing in adoption and the needs of children and their families."

-**DALE ROBIN GROSS**, M.F.T., Adoptive Mother and Psychotherapist

"Jeanette has created a revolution within the adoption community with her interventions. They encourage those touched by adoption to share their story, which in turn inspires countless others. What we have seen in our community is a powerful wave of change with boundless momentum. Together, under Jeanette's leadership, we will undoubtedly change the face of adoption."

-**CARRA GREENBERG**, Adult Adoptee and Adoption Attorney

Dedicated to all those in the
foster care and adoption constellation
near and far...

Introduction

Groundbreaking Interventions is comprised of creative treatment methods to be used with children and adolescents designed in an easy to use approach which makes therapy healing and fun. I have used these methods frequently in my work and am constantly adapting them to new children and circumstances. Using these ideas helps to bridge the gap between child and parent/therapist and create an environment of "play without pressure" and encourages children to develop a creative spirit, which instills hope and transformation. Children find the methods easy to use and understand because they are geared towards helping children interact, play, and learn.

The activities in this book came about by my own need to be more creative with children, especially those in foster care and adoption whom had many great difficulties and hurdles to overcome externally and internally. I found that through encouraging a child to create, it encourages a child to learn about themselves and the world around them. So I sought out and tested each idea in this book with different children. I would first begin with a child's interest and elaborate how I could tap into that resource so that the child could use it for them rather than against them. Resiliency is what I sought to create with each child. And found that they too, could transform shame, mistrust, and low self-esteem into pride, dependency and confidence.

The general aim of this book is to encourage creativity within the therapeutic relationship, break down the walls with children who have been highly traumatized and tap into a child's natural resources. I cover a wide range of topics and materials. The methods can be used with children and their parents at home or in therapy sessions: individually, in-group settings and in family therapy. Each method is clearly laid out so that the parent/therapist can choose an intervention for a particular set of symptoms, age range, learning skill, and type of therapy. All activities can be used for girls and boys ages 4 through 17.

An important note about using this book: certain items such as play-doh, large poster paper, clay, craft sticks, pipe cleaners and other miscellaneous items will have to be purchased beforehand in order to do the project successfully. I have included websites where you can purchase such items. I also encourage parents to explain the project to the child first and then follow the client's lead. Most of the methods follow a path of their own.

The Therapeutic Models who influence this book are Object Relations Theory, Attachment Focused Family Therapy, and Psychodynamic. A creative parent/therapist should be able to utilize any of the methods regardless of their modality.

I hope you find this book as useful and enjoyable as I have creating it!

I wish you all the best,
Jeanette Yoffe

Contents

SECTION I
Anxiety, Fear & Worry

PROJECT: SHADOW WORLD - PART I

AGE RANGE: 8-17 suggested.

GOAL: To create a place for the child to internalize as safe, fulfilling, where needs are met and gain a sense of control and empowerment over ones introjects.

SYMPTOM REDUCTION: Anxiety, worry, and fear.
SYMPTOM INCREASE: Self-awareness, self-esteem, empathy for oneself and others.

MATERIALS: 1 Large WHITE Oak tag poster paper
                          Pencil/Eraser
                          Markers-Colored

METHOD:

Child is introduced to the exercise as they are told they are going to create a Shadow World where they are the "boss" and they can have everything they have always wanted. Child is instructed to fold the Oak tag paper into 3 folds as to create a door. They are told to create a secret code on the door that only they know in order to enter which can include words, letters or numbers. Once the code is made the child is given the rules within the Secret World to create. They have 3 powers i.e. can fly, see through things, run fast, speak many languages, sense danger quickly, make things appear or disappear, or be invisible. There is 1 central castle with a king or queen (which is them). The king or queen can have 5 visitors; the child chooses who these are i.e. Family members, fictional characters or pets. There are 3 storage buildings, which will hold things in which they need i.e. food, clothing, toys, video games, ice cream etc. There is 1 wishing well which the child can go to in order to discard something bad that has snuck in the world and when the item is discarded into the well something good comes out in replace of it i.e. butterflies, candy bars, bubbles, etc. Once the rules are established the child is free to add on other items he/she needs to make it the most beautiful, perfect place.

TO PROCESS WITH CHILD/TEEN:

- This Shadow World is a place they can always go to when they feel unsafe in the real world.
- Sometimes in the outside world our needs will not always be met but we can create a safe place within us.
- There is a king or queen inside of you reminding you that life can be good, beautiful and fulfilling.
- You are in control of your world and scary emotions.

NOTES:

PROJECT: SHADOW WORLD - PART II

PREREQUISITE: The SHADOW World Part I

AGE RANGE: 8-17 suggested

GOAL: To create a place for the child to externalize and discover "rejected" parts of the self; i.e. shame, hate, fear, worry in order to create an awareness of these introjects and to gain a sense of control and empowerment over them rather than disowning them or fearing them.

SYMPTOM REDUCTION: Fear, worry, and anxiety.
SYMPTOM INCREASE: Self-awareness, self-esteem, empathy for self/others.

MATERIALS: 1 Large BLACK Oak tag poster paper
        Pencil/Eraser
        Markers-Gold or Silver

METHOD:

Child is introduced to the exercise as they are told they are going to create the second part of their Shadow World, which is "hidden" in his/her world that others cannot see. Again, the child is instructed to fold the Oak tag paper into 3 folds as to create the entrance door and told to create a secret code on the door that only they know in order to enter which can include words, letters or numbers. Once the code is made the child is again given the rules within the Shadow World to create. They have 3 powers (i.e. flying powers, force fields, invisibility, strength, or foresee the future). There is 1 central castle with a king or queen. The king or queen can have 5 visitors; the child chooses who these are such as family members, fictional characters or pets. In this world there are 3 gatekeepers within the central castle. There are 3 storage buildings, which will hold things in which they need in this Shadow World (i.e. armor, swords, weapons, etc.). There is 1 jail where the child can place things captive, which is bad or evil. There are 3 gatekeepers of the jail, which can be people, places or things. Once the rules are established the child is free to add in other items he/she needs to express that which is hidden and or protects him/her self-lurking in the darkness.

TO PROCESS WITH CHILD/TEEN:

- This Shadow World is that place which is hidden, unseen to our visitors but we must go inside to understand and know its powers so they don't overpower us.
- We can create order in the Shadow World because it can be very messy.
- When your light world inside turns to dark there is always a king or queen making sure what is there at all times to keep you safe.
- You can be in control of your world and scary emotions.

NOTES:

SECTION II
Anger, Aggression & Frustration

PROJECT: ANGER BAG™

AGE RANGE: 5-12 suggested

GOAL: To get child to utilize coping skills when he/she feels angry emotionally and/or physically in order to learn how to problem solve and regulate themselves on their own.

THERAPY: Individual and Family.

SYMPTOM REDUCTION: Feeling Angry, frustrated, and aggressive.
SYMPTOM INCREASE: Self-awareness, self-esteem, self-regulation, and self-reliance.

MATERIALS:
    1 Bag with Handles
    Scream Pillow
    Paper to rip or Old Phone Book
    Paper to draw with crayons
    Play-doh
    Bubble Wrap
    Bubbles
    8 Index Cards for Anger Busters
    Markers

METHOD:

Introduce the task by explaining to the child that he/she is going to help child gain control of these "angry" feelings with the use of a special bag they will explore and create together. Continue to explain that within the bag there will be special skills for him/her to do when they have these feelings and don't know how to express them. Order is not important.

Scream Pillow: The Scream pillow is used to help a child express their anger verbally. The parent/therapist/social worker can demonstrate first by placing their mouth in the middle of the pillow and start by making a sound of anger i.e. growl like a bear, roar like a lion, or scream as loud as they can all the while encouraging the child to try. As the child begins to feel more comfortable he/she can say words such as "I am angry" or "It's not fair" or "I am frustrated" or "I'm mad."

Paper to Rip: The child is told the "Paper to Rip" is available for him/her to rip up when they are frustrated or angry BUT the rule is when they are finished it must be cleaned up. As they rip up the paper the parent/therapist/social worker instructs the child to express why they are angry. The child can throw the paper up in the air or directly into a garbage pail. This can be very cathartic and freeing for a child. (See attached Paper to Rip Cover page for drawing book.)

Paper to Draw: The child is told the "Paper to Draw" is used to draw pictures about their anger with the Anger Buster Crayons. The child can draw pictures of the person and event and/or write words that express his/her anger. (See attached Paper to Draw Cover page for drawing book.)

Play-doh Rip-Squish-Spaghetti Technique: This technique teaches a child how to regulate and externalize their "angry" feelings. The child is instructed to open the play-doh, take out the play-doh and say out loud "RIP" while breaking it into 2 pieces. The child is then instructed to say the word "SQUISH" while squeezing his/her feelings into the play-doh, and then the child says "SPAGHETTI" while separating his fingers so that the play-doh squishes right through them like spaghetti. Tell the child to begin all over again with Rip-Squish-Spaghetti. He/she should do this 5-10 times until they feel more relaxed. Tell the child; this tool will help him/her release his or her angry feelings into the play-doh instead of somewhere else where someone may get hurt.

Anger Buster Poppers: This technique is always fun, safe and easy to use. The child can use the bubble wrap "poppers" to step on, stand on, sit on or jump on. This allows the child to project his/her aggression and/or hostile feelings in an expressive way. I encourage the child to tell me a story about what they are doing to the poppers and who the poppers represent to them.

Anger Buster Bubbles: The bubbles are used for blowing, of course. The child is instructed to sit down in a chair while performing this task. He/she is going to imagine seeing the angry feelings enter the bubble and then disappear when it pops. Encourage the child to focus, feel the lightness of the bubble gliding within their control. Each bubble he/she blows they watch until it pops, so that the child begins to regain focus and internalize a sense of calm.

Anger Buster Cards: The child with the help of the parent/therapist/social worker will create 3-8 Anger Busters and write coping skills on each card. The child is told he/she can reach in the bag and pick one out at anytime and they will tell him/her what to do with their anger.

Examples of Anger Busters are:

1. SCREAM as loud as I can in my SCREAM pillow! Ahhhhhhh!!!
2. PUNCH my SCREAM pillow with all MY might 10 times!!!!! Yippee!!!
3. TAKE 10 deep BREATHS –– IN and OUT of my BELLY!!! 1-2-3-4-5-6-7-8-9-10!!
4. SAY out LOUD 10 times "I AM THE BOSS OF MY ANGER!"
5. COUNT to 10 like this: 1 CHIMPANZEE, 2 chimpanzee, 3 chimpanzee, 4 chimpanzee, 5 chimpanzee, 6 chimpanzee, 7 chimpanzee, 8 chimpanzee, 9 chimpanzee, 10! Or CREATE my own WORD in between the numbers!
6. GO to MY mirror and make a FUNNY FACE!!! Don't forget to stick MY tongue out REALLY BIG!!!! Ahhh...
7. GO outside, FIND a stick and hit a TREE with all MY might... then HUG IT!!! Ahhh...8. DRAW a PICTURE or WORDS about the person or thing you are MAD at and WRIP IT UP to PIECES!!! Yowser!!!

At the end all of the items are placed back in the bag and the child or parent/therapist/social worker writes on the outside of the bag "Things to do when I feel angry to help me calm the pain inside me." The child keeps the bag within reach, hanging on a doorknob or hook in his/her room.

PAPER TO DRAW
A PICTURE
ABOUT
MY
"ANGRY"
FEELINGS!!!

PAPER TO
RIP
TO RELEASE
MY
"ANGRY"
FEELINGS!!!

PROJECT: ERUPT MY FEELINGS
- GO WITH MY FLOW

AGE RANGE: 4-17 suggested

GOAL: To get child to externalize repressed feelings of anger, loss and resentment towards others while projecting them into a volcanic eruption.

THERAPY: Individual and Family, 1-2 sessions.

SYMPTOM REDUCTION: Anger, aggressivity, and resentment.
SYMPTOM INCREASE: Sense of control, resiliency, and self-awareness.

MATERIALS: Modeling Clay
                  Aluminum tray
                  Thin glass tube or vase
                  Baking soda/Vinegar
                  Slips of paper & pen
                  Popsicle or people sticks

METHOD:

1st session: Explain to the child that you are going to help them with their overwhelming feelings by creating a volcano together and by erupting these feelings out. The first session will mainly be focused on constructing the volcano mold, which is done as such: the child is given the modeling clay with the aluminum tray and is told to construct the clay around the vase (which will be placed in the center). While the child is creating and molding the volcano, the parent/therapist can begin to process how the volcano will be used when it is finished by asking such questions as: what thoughts or feelings are boiling within the volcano that may want to be erupted out? What lies inside the volcano? Has this volcano erupted before? How old is this volcano? Where did the fire come from?

2nd session: The second session will consist of creating what will be erupted from the volcano by writing thoughts and ideas "that make them angry "down onto pieces of paper, which will then be placed into the mixture to erupt. Ask the child what feelings or thoughts are boiling inside of you?" Then instruct the child to write these feelings and thoughts down on paper to be placed in the inner tube. After the child does this, they are placed in the inner tube. Then put 1 tbsp. of Baking Soda to 1/4 cup of Vinegar. And while watching the eruption, you can process with the child "what it means to see your feelings/thoughts erupt." Ask questions like, "It must feel good to express and release those feelings/thoughts you have been holding onto inside and get them out.... Good erupting you are doing.... You must feel a sense of relief.... Let's do this again, and again...until you do... What else needs to be released?... what/who are you angry at?... what/who are you frustrated with?.... let's put it on a paper or popsicle stick and release it out....." I also like to use Popsicle sticks instead of paper because they stick out more and can be used as people. I had a child once use a Popsicle stick in the volcano that representing his drug-addicted biological father he loved very much who was abandoning him over and over. The child chose to erupt him over and over in the volcano while verbalizing his anger, which was quite a cathartic experience for this child.

NOTES:

PROJECT: MOTHER MAY I
WITH HULA HOOPS

AGE RANGE: 5-15 suggested.

GOAL: To get child to instill boundaries, foster open/clear communication, and learn impulse control with self and others.

THERAPY: Individual, Family and Small group (max 6 players).

SYMPTOM REDUCTION: Impulsivity, aggressivity, poor impulse control and anxiety.
SYMPTOM INCREASE: Boundary setting, impulse control, and problem solving skills.

MATERIALS: Hula Hoops (as many as there are players, including parent)
Reward point chips (pennies, poker chips etc.)
Rule chart
Assortment of toys- stuffed animals, toy cars, dolls, and action figures, balls.

METHOD:

The parent/therapist/social worker places the hula-hoops down on the ground and each child or family member picks a hula-hoop and is instructed to sit inside them. All sorts of toys are laid out around the hula-hoops for all to see but are told they cannot touch them until the game begins. The parent/therapist/social worker is given the reward point chips and serves as "the Mother." The child is told this is the Mother May I, Hula Hoops game where they are going to earn points for stopping, relaxing, and thinking. A good idea is to create an incentive for the child, for example if they earn 30 points they will earn a "special time with parent" (this is discussed with the parent), which could be i.e. make ice cream sundaes together, go for a bike ride together, etc. Then the child is given the rules of the game.

(See attached Rules List) The points can be changed depending upon the behavior you want to target. I will give a few examples for you.

An example of a Rules Chart is as follows (for children who are too young to read you can put symbols of a person doing that action):

NOTES:

"MOTHER MAY I" RULES

a. Each player must say "Mother May I" when beginning each turn.
(*2 points suggested*)

b. Ask for a toy and wait for the answer "yes" or "no."
(*1 point suggested*)

c. Accepting a "no" answer with no talking back.
(*5 points suggested*)

d. Give a toy to another player.
(*2 points suggested*)

e. Give kind words to another player.
(*5 points suggested*)

f. Use eye contact when speaking.
(*10 points suggested*)

g. Say thank you and please.
(*5 points suggested*)

h. Staying in your space in the hula-hoop.
(*10 points suggested*)

<u>Mother May I with Hula Hoops Continued:</u>

Each category represents important skills for children to learn: listening, following instructions, sharing, giving, engaging, respecting and maintaining self-control.

After the child chooses their action they are asked what they earned points for, which creates and instills an "awareness of self" and actions taken. Most children tend to really enjoy this game. The hula-hoops give them a container in order to feel secure, and the rules give them a structure to adhere to all the while earning and being rewarded for their efforts. This game is especially useful with children who have major control issues and create intense power struggles with parents. I have seen dramatic results with children of this nature who have been able to stop impulsivity and think before their actions.

<u>To Note: Teaching Boundaries with Hula Hoops:</u>

The idea of the hula-hoop began when I was wondering how to teach children about the concept of boundaries. As part of the Mother May I game I do an educational piece, telling children that we are surrounded by our own hula hoops meaning we all have "imaginary hula hoops in the world" and no one can enter our hula hoops without our permission and we cannot enter other people's hula hoops without their permission. So when playing the game, I encourage the child to notice how big their hula-hoops are, how much space they have around them and the space around others to understand the concept of personal space, where they end and others begin. Children are able, after explaining this concept, to understand personal boundaries for themselves and others.

SECTION III
Grief, Loss, & Depression

PROJECT: ANIMAL ADOPTION
(Foster Care, Foster-Adopt)

AGE RANGE: 5-12 suggested.

GOAL: To get child to adopt or foster an animal into their home, create a narrative of the animal's life, while projecting and connecting with their own feelings of grief and loss.

THERAPY: Individual and Family.

SYMPTOM REDUCTION: Shame, loneliness, abandonment, and lack of identity.
SYMPTOM INCREASE: Empathy, self-pride, accomplishment, confidence, and love.

MATERIALS: Stuffed Animal- Dog or Cat or Bear
                         Adoption birth certificate
                         Paper
                         Markers

METHOD:
Introduce child to the stuffed animal with a name. Explain to the child that the animal has been separated from their biological family and needs a home to live in and/or be adopted. Ask child if they are willing to adopt/foster the animal. With the parents help, begin to create a birth certificate and story for the lost animal to give them an identity with items such as:

Name:
Age:
Brothers/Sisters:
Homes lived in:
Why are they here?
What happened to them?
Foods he/she likes to eat?
My favorite things to do?

The worst things to do?
What he/she needs most?
Feelings they have?

Once this is done, have the child, parent, and caretaker officially sign the birth certificate and identified information document. Ask the child to hug the animal and officially accept him into the family. You can encourage the child to create a place for them to sleep, introduce them to their new room and show them around the house etc. (See attached Animal Adoption Certificate.)

PROJECT: HOLD ONTO MY FEELINGS

AGE RANGE: 4-17 suggested.

GOAL: To provide opportunity for family to create a safe and warm holding environment, build trust and secure the attachment.

SYMPTOM REDUCTION: Lack of trust/safety, reactive attachment, & anxiety.
SYMPTOM INCREASE: Trust, love, bonding, and attachment.

MATERIALS: Old Phone Book
                    New Pillowcase
                    Permanent Markers

METHOD:

To begin, the intervention can be introduced by therapist/parent as "We have noticed you have been holding onto a lot of 'feelings' and wanted to give you a way to release these feelings by letting you rip up this old phone book. And guess who is going to clean up and hold onto all of the feelings??? Not you, we are." The therapist/parent then playfully entices the child to participate by demonstrating the task first i.e. opening the phone book, ripping out a few pages at a time, ripping or smashing the paper apart or together, stating an example of what they are feeling such as "I'm mad because I can't drink soda for breakfast!!" and/or by showing their frustration/anger/pain without words via their facial cues by throwing the pages up in the air and watching them fall down. Making it seem fun and cathartic is the critical element that gets children to begin the process of releasing their pent up feelings. It is strongly suggested that therapists/parents encourage the child to say words associated with their feelings to help them build emotional intelligence by teaching "I" messages. "I feel _____ because _____." But do not force the child if they are non-verbal, their resistance may be a signal that they are not ready emotionally or are not feeling safe enough to verbalize at this time. Also, I recommend beginning the intervention with light-hearted feelings and complaints, allowing the child to feel comfortable with the process before digging in to more painful core issues.

I cannot stress enough how important it is to create an environment of safety. To do this it is important for therapists/parents to be very aware of their own state of being and not to be reactive. When successful, this intervention brings up many deep and repressed emotions and feelings that can be painful and even shocking to hear. Sometimes a child might say, "I wish I was never adopted", or "You're not my real parents". Let the child express their feelings without criticism, rejection, anger or dismissal. It is also important to keep in mind how one's own <u>non-verbal</u> facial expressions, and actions read to others. It is suggested to keep an open, stress free face, be overly curious (raised eyebrows), and breathe deeply during the exercise to help calm down and regulate any arousal states the child brings out in order to stay connected. Therapists/Parents are encouraged to enjoy the child's process by "oohing" and "aaahhing" with amazement as the child rips up the paper. This is a necessary part of the intervention as active and verbal support keeps the parent connected and engaged wile simultaneously increasing the levels of the oxytocin hormone, essential for bonding.

A good tip is to bring a small journal or notebook into the intervention. If, as a therapist/parent, you are becoming deregulated and/or overwhelmed, take a moment to write down what it is that is triggering you and you can revisit those notes at a later time. Remember, this exercise purposely manifests painful feelings in order to allow for a stronger emotional connection and feeling of trust.

If the child is resisting, some prompting is appropriate. I encourage therapists/parents of a reluctant child to ask, "Would you be willing to let mommy or daddy speak a feeling you have said before so we can feel it together?" i.e. "I'm mad because I don't see my biological mother!" "I'm sad because we don't look alike." "I'm sad because I didn't grow in your tummy!" "I'm sad because you are not my real mother." "I'm mad because I have so many feelings and I feel so overwhelmed!" Doing this often entices the child to participate.

Don't feel the need to rip up the entire phone book or solve every painful issue in one session. A good time to "stop" is after an emotional epiphany or a particularly positive exchange. Or if you've been proceeding for 45 minutes and the child seems to be avoiding the deeper issues. You can get to them at another time. When you've sensed they've had enough or they tell you they're done ripping the paper, instruct the child to take a comfy seat somewhere in the room and "supervise" as you, the parents, begin to "pick up all the feelings." (Be careful not to say "time to pick up the garbage!") However, before you begin to pick up the "feelings" take a moment and breathe... Look at the scattered papers around the room and see them as your child's "emotional life." I usually make a statement such as, "Wow look at all these feelings!!! They sure can get messy. Are feelings messy sometimes? Thank you for letting me know. Now, I am going to give them all the love and care that they deserve."

As the child observes, the parent takes the pillowcase and begins to pick up each feeling, either in piles or single pieces and comment on them with great empathy as you do so... "I'm sorry too that you do not see your biological mother." "I'm sorry too that we do not look alike." "I'm sorry too that your biological mommy could not be your everyday mommy." "This feeling I am going to hold on to and give lots of love."

It is strongly suggested that parents do what they feel is authentic in their hearts at this moment. I have witnessed parents kiss each paper and not say much at all, hug piles of feelings and convey to the child through facial expressions "how much this means to them", and have witnessed many parents reduced to tears upon truly understanding the depth of their child's grief. Or realizing, in these moments, that it is their responsibility to feel these emotions along with their child and not simply deny them. I've also seen many children's faces light up and be amazed at their parents' capacity to be so reflective, open and honest about the reality of their adoption and the realization that they are truly loved. This intervention is a bridge toward healing and attachment for many of the families I have worked with and continue to work with.

In the end, when all the "feelings" have been identified and placed in the pillowcase, ask the child, "Are there any feelings I have missed?" The child scans the room and points them out so all have been acknowledged. Then the parents write a closing response on the bag such as "I understand." "I love all of your feelings." "I am here to listen." "I want to help hold on to your sadness, so you don't have to hold on all by yourself." The parent then reads the response out loud to the child and lets the child know, "We are going to hold on to these feelings until you tell me to let go of them. I will keep them close to our bed and keep them safe." Parent is instructed to carry the "bag of feelings" around the house some times, this act conveys to the child their feelings can be secured and their parents can handle them and will not be overwhelmed by them.

PROJECT: MY JOURNEY THROUGH PLACEMENT

AGE RANGE: 8-12 suggested.

GOAL: To get child to create a narrative about their foster and/or adoption story, sequence their life events while gaining understanding and awareness.

THERAPY: Individual & Family.

SYMPTOM REDUCTION: Post-traumatic stress worries, fear, and shame
SYMPTOM INCREASE: Confidence, self-compassion, and objectivity.

MATERIALS: Popsicle Sticks
Pipe Cleaners (equal amount as sticks)
Markers or crayons
String
Cardboard cut in the shape of a house (as many as their placements)
Whole Puncher
2 chairs to tie string across
Construction paper
Scissors

METHOD:

Explain to child and/or family that together you are going to create a show about his/her life. The child is instructed to make a Popsicle stick person of him/her self first using the markers to color in his face, hair, body etc. Then they are told to make the people in his/her 1st family by using the Popsicle sticks as each person. Then take a pipe cleaner and hook it around the middle part of each Popsicle stick so that a hook remains on top, which will later be hooked onto the string. The child is instructed to continue to make the persons in his 2nd, 3rd or 4th family (as many placements as he/she can remember). Also, do not forget his current placement, as that is the end of the play. As the child is doing this, the parent/therapist designates each placement family a house. The child can also color and design the homes as he/she remembers them. When the people and houses are done the parent/therapist will place a hole (w/whole puncher) on the top of each house, place the houses on the string, in the order of placements and tie the string between 2 chairs as to create a string of houses. The child is instructed to place the people who belong in each house in front of the homes by hooking them on the line. The child then takes him/herself and places them on the line at the beginning. The parent/therapist will guide the child through their story and multiple placements by asking such questions as: "Where did you begin your journey?" "What do you remember about that home/family?" "What was the best part?" "What was the worst part?" "Where did you move next?" "What happened that you had to move?" "What was it like in your new home?" The story continues until he/she ends up at current placement.

Purchase People Popsicle Sticks at *www.LakeshoreLearning.com*

NOTES:

PROJECT: MY QUESTIONS & ANSWERS BOX

AGE RANGE: 4-17 suggested.

GOAL: To get child to externalize unanswered questions about his/her life in foster care and adoption and also provide a container for their anxiety.

SYMPTOM REDUCTION: Anxiety, helplessness, and confusion.
SYMPTOM INCREASE: Empowerment, understanding, and self-esteem.

MATERIALS: 2 boxes of any kind with tops
Small sheets of paper
Pen or pencil
Materials to decorate box, colored paper, fabric, stickers

METHOD:

Introduce the first box to the child as the "Question Box" which is going to hold all of the child's questions about their life that he/she has always had. Introduce the second box as the "Answers Box" which is going to hold any answers found out about their life. The child is encouraged to decorate and name each special box for themselves as to create significance and importance. The child is then instructed to write questions down on the pieces of paper and place them in to the Question box. It is important to tell the child that "sometimes we will never know all the answers but we at least have a place to hold the questions other than inside us all the time to help carry the load." The box may be shown to a parent, social worker or the child's attorney or any professional who may have answers about the child's past. The answers can be placed in the Answers Box for the child to read or in their Life Book. Examples of questions are:

Why am I in foster care?
What happened to my mommy or daddy?
Do I have any brothers or sisters?
Why did my mommy give me up?

Where is my mommy now?
Who is my daddy?
Can I get a picture of my mommy or daddy?
If the child has had multiple placements:
What happened to my foster family?
Is this my forever family?
Can I write a letter to my foster family?
Why couldn't they keep me?

NOTES:

PROJECT: SAD BAG

<u>AGE RANGE:</u> 5-12 suggested

<u>GOAL:</u> To get child to utilize coping skills when he/she feels sad emotionally in order to learn how to problem solve and regulate themselves on their own.

<u>SYMPTOM REDUCTION:</u> Feeling sad, depressed, or hopeless.
<u>SYMPTOM INCREASE:</u> Self-awareness, self-esteem, self-regulation, and self-reliance.

<u>MATERIALS:</u>   1 Bag with Handles
Tear Pillow
Magical Wish Journal
Paper to draw with crayons
Small Photo Album
1 pack of Guatemalan Worry Dolls
Bubbles
8 Index Cards for Sad Busters
Markers

<u>METHOD:</u>

Introduce the task by explaining to the child that he/she is going to help child gain control of these "sad" feelings with the use of a special bag they will explore and create together. Continue to explain that within the bag there will be special skills for him/her to do when they have these feelings and don't know how to express them. Order is not important.

Tear Pillow: The Tear pillow is used to help a child express their sadness verbally and to be used for self comfort and care. The parent/therapist/ social worker can demonstrate first by placing their face in the middle of the pillow and start by making sounds of sadness i.e. sighing, boo-hoo-ing, pretending to cry, all the while encouraging the child to try. Then as the child begins to feel more comfortable he/she can say words such as "I am sad" or "It's not fair" or "I am hurt" or "I feel sad."

Magical Wish Journal: The journal is used as a diary to express sad feelings. The child is told that the Magical journal can bring magic into their life when they write down their wishes. Whenever they write their wishes into their journal amazing things will happen, the angels will hear them and angels can only listen to Magic Wish journals. Sometimes so many angels hear them and their wishes come true.

Paper to Draw: The child is told the "Paper to Draw" is used to draw pictures about their sad feelings. The child can draw pictures of the person and event and/or write words, which express his/her pain. (See attached Paper to Draw Cover page for drawing book.)

Small Photo Album: This is used for the child to put pictures of people and/or things that make him/her happy. This can be "real" pictures of loved ones in their life or pictures of persons/places/things from magazines i.e. cartoon characters, flowers, funny pictures. The child can title the album i.e. "Things that make me smile" "The people who love me in my life." "I am always loved." "I can be happy."

1 pack of Guatemalan Worry Dolls: These are used for the child to express their concerns, worries and fears into an external object. I like to introduce the dolls as "powerful Friends," who can help us with our feelings but we have to tell them what we are upset about one by one so that they can discuss it that evening. The "powerful friends" must be placed under their pillow while they are sleeping and if they listen really hard they can hear them talking their sadness away and when they wake up in the morning they will feel better.

Bubbles Blow-away-disappear technique: The bubbles are used for blowing, of course. The child is instructed to sit down in a chair while performing this task. He/she is going to imagine seeing the stressful feelings enter the bubble and then disappear when it pops. Encourage the child to focus, feel the lightness of the bubble gliding within their control.

Each bubble he/she blows they watch until it pops, so that the child begins to regain focus and internalize a sense of calm.

Sad Busters: The child with the help of the parent/therapist/social worker will create 3-8 Sad Busters and write them on the card. These are also stored in the bag and the child is told he/she can reach in the bag and pick one out at anytime and they will tell him/her what to do with their stress.

Examples of Sad Busters are:

1. CROSS my ARMS around my body and give myself a big, BIG HUG!!!
2. SAY the TONGUE twister: "Silly sally, sang dilly dallies sitting on a swing." OUT LOUD 10 times!!!
3. CRY on my Tear Pillow and let the RAINBOW catch my TEARS for me!!!
4. TAKE 5 deep breathes SLOWLY.
5. WRITE my SAD feelings in my JOURNAL.
6. ASK my parent for a HUG!!!
7. GO to MY mirror and make a funny face REALLY BIG!!!
8. GO get my BUBBLES and BLOW 3 wishes into the air!!!

At the end all of the items are placed back in the bag and the child or parent/therapist/social worker writes on the outside of the bag "Things to do when I feel sad to make my broken heart feel glad!" The child keeps the bag within reach, hanging on a doorknob or hook in his/her room.

PAPER TO DRAW
A PICTURE
ABOUT
MY
"SAD"
FEELINGS!!!

PROJECT: CANDLE RITUAL

AGE RANGE: 13-17 suggested.

NOTE: THIS INTERVENTION MUST BE SUPERVISED AND GRANTED PERMISSION BY THE PARENT TO DO SO AS THIS USES MATCHES/FIRE.

GOAL: To get teen to symbolize their biological family and their journey thus far.

SYMPTOM REDUCTION: Anxiety, helplessness, and confusion.
SYMPTOM INCREASE: Empowerment, understanding, and self-esteem.

MATERIALS: Candle/Matches
Stickers
Letter writing paper
Pencil or Pen
Aluminum Tin Pan and Matches

METHOD:

Introduce to the teen that they are going to create/decorate a candle and designate who the candle represents, "their biological mother or their biological father." Use the stickers to decorate the candle. Then with the supervision of an adult, light the candle and ask the teen to sit and bask in its warmth for a few minutes to make a connection. Then encourage the teen to begin to write a letter to one of their biological parents. Tell them to include everything they didn't get a chance to say or what they want to share with them now. This can include feelings of loss, sadness, regret, guilt, worry, fear, rage, joy, and words of thanks. It can be a story of what is happening in their life now. Or anything they want to share with them. When they are finished writing the letter, ask them to take a moment and read the letter out loud (twice). Then when they are ready they can light the letter on fire and place the letter into the aluminum pan while watching it burn into flames.

Process with Teen:

The physical action of giving life to your feelings by putting them into words (when you write the letter), hearing your own words (as you read the letter out loud)...and then finally, launch them into the universe (by tossing them into the fire) is symbolic of the permission you have given yourself to express your truth and then let it go, an opportunity for you to share your unsaid words, wishes, and feelings to your biological parent by launching them into the universe."

<u>NOTES:</u>

SECTION IV
Making Sense of My Story

PROJECT: MY STRING OF CONNECTIONS

AGE RANGE: 4-12 suggested.

GOAL: To provide opportunity for child to acknowledge/reflect all the connections they have had through their life's transitions.

SYMPTOM REDUCTION: Feeling disconnected, unloved, lacking object constancy, or lack of trust.
SYMPTOM INCREASE: Trust, love, connection, bonding, and attachment.

MATERIALS: Cut out hearts from construction paper (30-50)
                       1 Hole Punch & Tape
                       Yarn String, 3-6 feet
                       Pens and Markers

METHOD:

This is a wonderful intervention to help children re-connect and "visually see" all the connections of all the people who have been a part of their lives in their past and present. This exercise reassures them that they are loved and that they have loved and that "love is continuous and ongoing." This gives them a sense they are not alone, even if they are physically separated from loved ones, they learn they are always connected to them with the metaphor of an "invisible string."

Introduce to the child they are going to create "a string of connections" to recognize all the people who have been in their life whom "they feel/have felt a connection to." To begin the child is given a stack of cut out hearts and some pens and markers. The therapist then directs the child with the help of the parent to write one name on each heart. I usually start with their biological i.e. biological parents, adoptive parents, animals, relatives, friends at home and at school. If a child has a strong connection to places and things I encourage them to write a heart for each. Examples of places are connections to a birth country/state i.e. China, Texas. Examples of things are connections to a stuffed animal, or special item given to them by their biological parent.

As soon as the parent/child are finished each heart is given a single whole punch. A string is cut long enough to cover the width of the room in order to hang across from one side to the other. The hearts are then placed on the string with space between each one so the names are visible. Place tape at either end of the string and hang across the entire room. The child/parent can sit down and look up at all the connections they have had and have while reflecting/processing these connections with the child. The child takes the string home and places it up in their room so they can see "they are not alone" and "forever connected by a string."

NOTES:

PROJECT: MY FAMILY TREE

AGE RANGE: 5-13 suggested.

GOAL: To get child to create a narrative about their foster and/or adoption story, sequence their life events while gaining understanding and awareness.

SYMPTOM REDUCTION: Post-traumatic stress, confusion, worry, fear, and shame.

SYMPTOM INCREASE: Confidence, self-compassion, and objectivity.

MATERIALS: Poster Board
Tree stencil or can draw a tree free hand or tracing your hand with your arm as the trunk
As accurate a List of Placements the child has had with dates
Colored paper cut out in the shapes of houses (equal to # of placements)
Construction paper
Markers
Glue
Scissors

METHOD:

Explain to the child and/or family that together you are going to create a narrative about his/her life. The child is instructed to start at the bottom of the poster board to make a tree. The bottom tree is the biological family tree, their "roots." They are then instructed to write each biological family member's name on a leaf and add it to the tree. The next step is to continue above the biological family tree. The child is instructed to glue either another tree or a house to signify their next move. Again, they are instructed to write each foster family member's name on a leaf and add it to the tree. The child is instructed to continue to make the persons in his 2nd, 3rd or 4th family (as many placements as he/she can remember). Multiple poster boards can be taped together to keep the flow and consistency of the child's narrative. At each placement, it is important to write next to the tree or house, the dates the child lived there, the name of the family and any important information about the experience there. The child can also color and design the homes as he/she remembers them. When the mapping of the placements, tress and houses are done the child can continue to decorate, add photos, color feelings next to each family or write words to continue to process/express their thoughts/feelings. The parent/therapist/social worker will guide the child through their story and multiple placements by asking such questions as: "Where did you begin your journey?" "What do you remember about that home/family?" "What was the best part?" "What was the worst part?" "Where did you move to next?" "What happened that you had to move?" "What was it like in your new home?" The story continues until he/she ends up at their current placement.

NOTES:

PROJECT: THE PARTS OF ME

AGE RANGE: 5-17 suggested.

GOAL: To get child to externalize painful and overwhelming feelings of trauma and loss in an objective, creative and constructive way by sorting out in an art collage their "emotional" parts.

SYMPTOM REDUCTION: Grief, helplessness, splitting, post-traumatic stress.

SYMPTOM INCREASE: Objectivity, Self-esteem, Confidence, and Resiliency.

MATERIALS: 1 Large White Poster Paper
Small Envelopes
Index cards that fit in the envelopes
Glue/Markers

METHOD:

Child/Teen is told they will be creating and discovering the "many feeling parts" within them in order to make sense, understand, and help them grow. Ask the child, as the therapist/parent, to draw their body very large covering the entire poster board.

1. Then direct the child to draw a circle, which represents their "happy" part, and ask them to color this in. Then glue an envelope to the happy part and write on the index cards what the happy part says, i.e. "I am happy because I love my mom" "I am happy when I eat ice cream." "I am happy because I am loved." Etc.

2. Then direct the child to draw a circle, which represents their "unhappy" part, and ask them to color this in. Then again, glue an envelope to the unhappy part and write on the index cards what the unhappy part says, i.e. "I am unhappy because I miss my foster mom." "I am unhappy because I get so mad sometimes."

3. Now go back to the "happy" part and ask that part how they can help the unhappy part, ask "what "action" does the unhappy part need to do to be more happy?" And write this down on a card and place it in the "unhappy" envelope. I.e. "I can write my feelings down or jump on my bean bag pillow to get happy again."

This 3-step protocol is the process which is used to identify any/all feelings a child/teens may have and help them work through any shame they may have about that feeling by breaking it down into many parts. It is important to be direct when approaching this exercise by explaining to the child/teen-

1. When we have a feeling, there is a part of us that is "unhappy" and there is another part that is "happy."
2. There is a part of us that may feel bad, AND there is another part that feels "good about myself" which can help me with my "feeling bad part."
3. There is a part of me that may feel sad, AND there is another part that feels "at peace" which can help my "sad part" feel better.

NOTES:

SECTION V
Building Family Attachment & Bonding

PROJECT: "I MESSAGE" EGG HUNT

AGE RANGE: 4-16 suggested.

GOAL: To provide opportunity for family to convey loving messages to one another and create a safe and warm holding environment, build trust and secure the attachment.

SYMPTOM REDUCTION: Lack of trust/safety, reactive attachment, & anxiety.
SYMPTOM INCREASE: Trust, love, bonding, and attachment.

MATERIALS: 12 Plastic Easter Eggs
                   Small Pieces of paper & Pen

METHOD:

This is an attachment intervention to help children feel and know they are loved, acknowledged and validated within their family, and feel safe enough to give love in return. Introduce to the family that they are going to "write I messages" on paper, fold them up, put the message in an egg to and hide them in the room for the child to find. An "I message" must be positive and be given as a form of love. The following are examples to give you an idea:

"I love it when you tell me how your day at school was."
"I appreciate you when you help me with the groceries."
"I love your smile."
"I care about your feelings."
"I care about what you think."
"I love you, in my heart you'll always be, here or there, near or far my love will be there wherever you are!"
"I notice what a great friend you are."
"I love being in love with you!"
"I see how hard you are working at school."
"I thank you for caring for grandma when she was sick."

"I appreciate you doing your chores, you are a great help around the house."

Most kids enjoy this game of searching because they know the reward is positive! While the parents are writing their messages the child can look at a book or draw OR do their own messages for the parents if they wish. When the parents have finished writing their messages, the child hides their eyes, while the parent hides the eggs in the room. Then the child is directed to go on a scavenger hunt around the room playing the "hot, cold" game while the parent(s) are giving them some direction by yelling out, "hot" when they get close to an egg and "cold" when they stray far away. Once an egg is found the child opens it up, hands it to the parent to read it to them "face to face." This is a wonderful exchange of love through effortless play!

NOTES:

PROJECT: PROTECT MY HEART

AGE RANGE: 4-17 suggested.

GOAL: To provide opportunity for family to establish a deeper connection, build trust and reinforce love and safety.

SYMPTOM REDUCTION: Feeling unloved, unimportant and lack of trust.

SYMPTOM INCREASE: Trust, bonding, and attachment.

MATERIALS: Model Magic, Blue & YellowRolling pinBook "*I Love You Through and Through*" by Bernadette Rossetti-Shustak

METHOD:

This is a wonderful intervention to help children/teen learn to trust their family and know that they are loved and secure in their attachment to them. Introduce to the family that they are going to create each of their hearts. To begin each parent is given an equal amount of YELLOW play-doh and the child is given a smaller amount of BLUE play-doh. Each member is encouraged to make their heart in whatever shape they see it. Once the play-doh is shaped, the therapist then directs the child to carefully place their heart on top of their parent's heart. The parent is then instructed to wrap their heart around the child's heart with great care. The therapist encourages the parent(s) to verbalize how they will care for their child's heart i.e. "I will keep his/her heart warm, protect his/her heart from harm, I will console their heart when it is aching." The therapist can help the parent verbalize this for the parent as well and can add, "His/hers heart has been broken and hurts so badly. This heart is tough and needs so much love and warmth and cuddles and kisses for a long, long time. Can you love his/her heart for a long, long time… through and through no matter what?" The parent(s) respond with great empathy and understanding for the child's hurts as they continue to knead and blend their heart around the child's by responding i.e. "I will love and warm and cuddle his/her heart and be very gentle." When this is completed the therapist asks the child if he/she has any empty feelings or missing pieces in their heart i.e. missing family members, lost memories. The child is encouraged to poke holes in their blue heart for the parent to fill with parts from their yellow heart. Sometimes the child likes to fill these holes by them self, encourage the child to let the parent fill these holes for them and verbalize to the child that they "can let love in and out of their heart, and that the love from their parents heart is safe and warm." The parent is then instructed to read to the child the book "*I Love You Through and Through.*"

NOTES:

PROJECT: WRAP ME UP IN LOVE

AGE RANGE: 4-17 suggested.

GOAL: To provide opportunity for family to create a safe and warm holding environment, build trust and secure the attachment.

SYMPTOM REDUCTION: Lack of trust/safety, reactive attachment, & anxiety.
SYMPTOM INCREASE: Trust, love, bonding, and attachment.

MATERIALS: Toilet Paper 2 double rolls
Wrapping Paper & Bows & stickers
Chair/Hand Fan
Snacks-Juice boxes/cookies/fruit

METHOD:

This is an attachment intervention to help children feel contained emotionally within their family, feel loved, physically safe and secure and give love in return. Introduce to the family that they are going to "wrap each other up in toilet paper" one at a time. Most kids think this is hilarious! This intervention is quite enticing and most kids want "to be wrapped" first. Also, what the child doesn't know is as they are being wrapped in toilet tissue the parent is going to verbalize how much they love the child and express how safe they will keep the child. What this exercise ends up mirroring is what it must feel like to be a fetus in a womb, ever safe and ever warm.

To begin, the family member whom will be doing the wrapping will be given 1 roll of toilet paper. The other will sit in the seat. The one who wraps will begin with the feet and move their way up the body. As the family member wraps, they are instructed to verbalize what they are wrapping the person in i.e. warmth, a web, happiness, love, etc. The parent/therapist/ social worker will ask the one who is being wrapped asking if they are thirsty or hungry and directs the person wrapping to give them what they need. The parent/therapist/social worker will also ask "how does it feel to be wrapped in love, happiness, warmth etc.?"

To note: when the wrapper reaches the face, the face is not to be covered as to allow breathing openly unless the participant requests otherwise.

To finish, the wrapper will complete the exercise by adding stickers, bows, fanning the one being wrapped, checking in to see how they feel and what they need i.e. Juice Box, snack, a love sticker. Once the wrap is complete the parent/therapist/social worker tells the one who is wrapped that they will count to 3 and on 3 they can break free from the toilet paper. Children love the entrapment and the escape all the same. I have done this exercise with many children and have toilet paper on hand at all times because they request to do this over and over. This exercise allows for a "womb like experience" of feeling safe and secure and fosters unconditional love between parent and child.

NOTES:

PROJECT: MY CALM SPACE

AGE RANGE: 4-12 suggested.

GOAL: To get child to internalize a sense of safety in their world, initiate self-control and provide a container for their anxiety, fears and/or helplessness.

SYMPTOM REDUCTION: Dysregulation, anxiety, and helplessness.
SYMPTOM INCREASE: Regulation, understanding, and self-empathy.

MATERIALS: 1 Large box which child can fit in with tops/ designated spot in room
Markers, crayons
Materials to decorate box, colored paper, fabric, stickers

METHOD:

Introduce the box to the child as a "Calm Box" or "Safe Place" in which they can go to in order to feel safe and secure in the world when the outside world feels unsafe and insecure. Further describe how this box will help them calm down and be peaceful with the use of special items chosen to live in there. Teach the child the words "regulation" and "dysregulation" as to help them understand their own needs. Rules for the box include: only the child is allowed in the box and only they can choose what goes in and out of it. Encourage child to think of things they could use while being in their "safe calm box." Examples to include are: soft pillows, blankets, flashlight, radio, paper/crayons, favorite stuffed animals, food container for crackers or cookies, water bottle, pacifier, baby bottle, books, and pictures.

Designate where this box will go in their home, usually their room. The child is encouraged to decorate their box inside and out, create an entry, re-name this box for themselves as to create significance and importance.

APPENDIX I

10 Intervention Tips for Bonding & Attaching with Foster and Adopted Children:

Connecting Through the Senses: Hearing, Sight, Touch, Smell, and Taste

1. Read books that focus on the child-parent relationship.

   a. *I Love You Forever,* by Robert Munsch and Sheila McGraw
   b. *I Love You So Much,* by Carl Norac and Claude K. Dubois
   c. *Hug,* by Jez Alborough
   d. *I Like it When…*by Mary Murphy
   e. *Why I Need You,* by Gregory Lang and Janet Lankford-Moran
   f. *I Love You All Day Long,* by Francesca Rusackas and Priscilla Burris

2. Utilize physical affection as much as possible. This will restructure the brain and create positive endorphins to the body. Be very playful to lessen the fear of closeness.

   • Soft touches on arms, pats on the back.
   • 20-second hugs daily begin the brain's process of releasing the oxytocin hormone, which is necessary for bonding.
   • Steal kisses, steal tickles, and rock together.
   • Suggest a massage daily, or suggest washing child's hands.
   • Fall into each other. Play "cowboys and Indians" and as you are attacking each other fall onto the child gracefully as opposed to falling away.
   • Give a back rub with your back to each other. Sitting back to back, movement is "animal like" rubbing into each other to feel each other and hear each other. Play with what the child gives you and give it back in return.

3. Create "Experience Books" of child and parent doing positive and fun activities together. I.e. Our trip to Florida, Disneyland, Lego land with mommy, Sea World with Daddy. Read and share positive memories of the event together.

4. Adopt a stuffed animal that becomes a part of the family and is treated with nurturance, has an adoption or foster care certificate which contracts the commitment that you are making to this new member of the family. Spray

5. Have children's music playing to foster closeness with singing between you and your child. I.e. bands such as Elizabeth Mitchell, Billy Zane, and Sugarland.

6. Utilize "I love you stamps" or heart stickers, which can be placed on a child's body in a place where only the child and parent know where it is to create closeness.

7. Create a "Calm Box" (large refrigerator/Appliance box) or "Safe Place" (blanket over a table) with child to acknowledge there is a "place of emotional safety" to go to when the world outside seems overwhelming. Include books/paper/dolls/nurturing items that can soothe child.

8. Create "Family Wish Book" where each family member can enter wishes/wants and a family member can surprise that person with the wish at any time.

9. Have free play with parent one on one with child daily, a certain amount of time is allotted with no interruptions. Child chooses the activity. To create structure, have a list of games to choose from.

- Play board games, building with blocks, and puzzles.
- Play doctor or nurse to each other. Have real Band-Aids available for pretend wounds and have an attitude of great empathy and sorrow for the wounds.

- Play "baby and mommy" together, allow the regression to occur, utilize soft blankets/pillows. I recommend dog blankets they are made of the softest material. Pretend feeding with a bottle, have lots of holding the child like a baby, rocking, singing to, and coddling.
- Draw an "island" together on a large sheet of paper for only the parent and child to love on with all of their favorite things.
- Bake Cookies together and then enjoy eating/feeding them to each other.
- Do Face Painting. Parent and child take turns painting each other's faces.
- Buy "String Licorice" and measure different parts of the child's body and say, "This is how big your smile is" then feed the licorice to the child.
- Have a Staring Contest. Child and parent sit cross-legged touching knees. Adult puts his hands on the child's shoulders; child puts his hands on parent's arms. Adult says, "When I say Go we have to look in each other's eyes. The last person to blink wins, and gets the prize, he can give the other guy a hug or a tickle."
- Hide Easter Eggs Around the House with "I love you" messages and have the child find them.

10. Create transitional objects for child to hold when there is separation I.e. keychain with parents picture, necklace with locket, piece of clothing of parents that is recognizable, picture of parent and child together!

You can order a DVD and/or download individual interventions of Jeanette Yoffe showing you hands on how to utilize these Groundbreaking Interventions. Please visit her at http://www.CeliaCenter.org

"To meet the needs of children we need to be patient, be present, and be willing to provide opportunities to play. When we stay innocent and let go of our egos, we ultimately will heal our own "inner child" and continue on the lifelong journey of becoming whole."
—Jeanette Yoffe, M.F.T.

NOTES

Made in the USA
Monee, Il
18 October 2020

45431829R00049